GRADE TWO

MICHAEL AARON
PIANO COURSE
LESSONS

Especially designed to create student interest and progress by combining basic elements of piano technic with melody.

Alfred Music
P.O. Box 10003
Van Nuys, CA 91410-0003
alfred.com

ISBN-10: 0-89898-859-4
ISBN-13: 978-0-89898-859-8

PREFACE

The simple and direct approach which characterized GRADE ONE of this course, has been incorporated in the design of GRADE TWO. Below is an outlined plan of this book.

OUTLINE PLAN OF GRADE TWO

MELODIC MATERIAL

Original melodic material, especially composed to carry out a definite and progressive pedagogical plan. Easy arrangements of the Masters to awaken a desire to know more of the great music literature.

NOTE READING TESTS

To facilitate note reading, the student is asked to spell out words by writing the correct letter name of each note, in specially designed tests. These have been extended to include leger lines and spaces. These little games add interest to an important phase of music study.

PEDAL STUDIES

As the average student is inclined to experiment with the pedal, much to the annoyance of the family and the neighbors, it was deemed necessary to include Pedal Studies which clearly illustrate the correct usage of the pedal.

CONSTRUCTION OF MUSIC

Many aids in the form of Explanatory Charts give the student a knowledge of Theory, Harmony and the construction of music which is so essential to good musicianship.

DICTIONARY OF MUSICAL TERMS

The various musical terms used in this book are defined in the music dictionary on page 63.

In summation, the purpose and aim of this book is to build solidly on the foundation established in GRADE ONE, increase the technical facility of the student, stimulate his appreciation of music, and serve as a reliable guide and helpmate to the teacher.

Michael Aaron

CONTENTS

Thru Central Park

(Broken Chords)

Play this piece in a brisk and lively manner. The notes in the treble staff are composed of two broken chords. The notes in the bass staff are also composed of two broken chords.

Note Reading Tests

Leger Lines and Spaces Above Middle C and Below Middle C

In order to write music ABOVE or BELOW the staff, we add short lines and spaces called LEGER LINES and SPACES. The following chart shows how music may be written ABOVE or BELOW MIDDLE C without changing the CLEF signs.

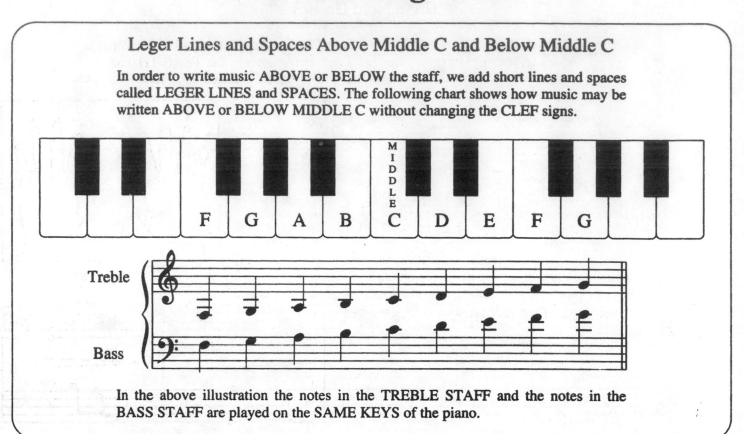

In the above illustration the notes in the TREBLE STAFF and the notes in the BASS STAFF are played on the SAME KEYS of the piano.

SPELL the words by writing the correct letter name of each note.

To complete each test you must play the correct notes on the piano.

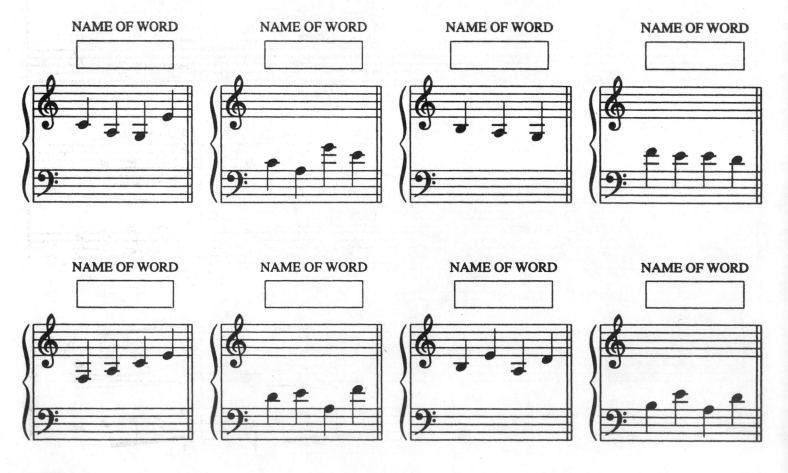

Five Finger Study

(Five Note Group)

In order to play music properly, it is essential to have a well developed hand. The first, second and third fingers of the hand are strong, while the FOURTH and FIFTH are usually weak. To strengthen the weak fingers, practice each five note group in the following manner:

Surf Riders

In the first measure of each line, cross the right hand over the left, BEFORE the left hand completes the measure. This will prepare your right hand for the next measure and help you keep a smooth, even tempo.

9

Inversions of Triads

The word INVERSION means a change of order or position.

C MAJOR TRIAD

In GRADE ONE we studied the first or ROOT POSITION

C (the ROOT) at BOTTOM

Now place C (the ROOT of the chord) on top,
and you have FIRST INVERSION

C (the ROOT) on TOP

Place E (the 3rd of the chord) on top,
and you have SECOND INVERSION

C (the ROOT) in the MIDDLE

Here are the three positions in one measure.

C Major Triad

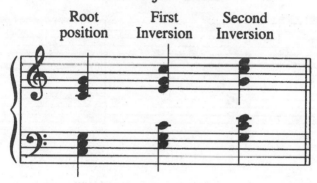

Chord Study in Inversions

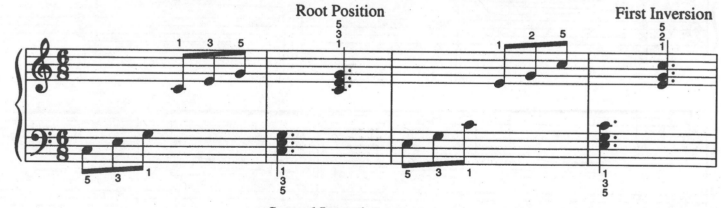

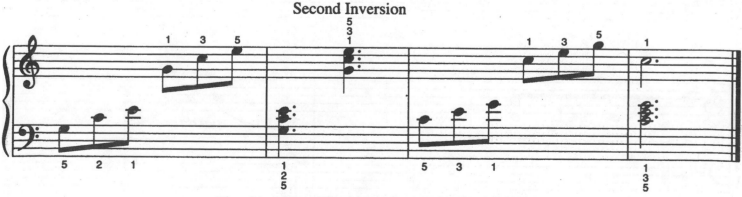

The above Chord Study may be practiced in all keys.

Song Without Words

To develop a good SINGING TONE, play with a "heavy arm" and "clinging fingers."

Andante cantabile

Note Reading Tests

(Leger Lines and Spaces Above the Treble and Below the Bass)

Spell the words by writing the correct letter name of each note.

To complete each test you must play the correct notes on the piano

NAME OF WORD

NAME OF WORD

NAME OF WORD

NAME OF WORD

NAME OF WORD

NAME OF WORD

NAME OF WORD

NAME OF WORD

Spell the following words with the correct notes. Write on LEGER LINES and SPACES.

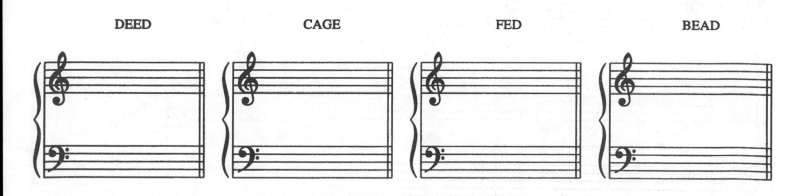

DEED

CAGE

FED

BEAD

Five Finger Study

(Nine Note Group)

FIRST TIME—Practice one note to the beat (quarters)

SECOND TIME—Practice two notes to the beat as written (eighths)

Syncopation

The normal accent in music is on the beat:

Count   1   2   3   4

SYNCOPATION is a shifting of the normal accent. When a long note is played on the weak part of the beat, a form of syncopation occurs.

Rhythm Pattern for "Show-Boat Ride"

Count 1 a 2 a 3 a 4 a   1 a 2 a 3 a 4 a

or   1 and 2 and 3 and 4 and etc.

Clap hands for each note and count aloud.

Show-Boat Ride

*Remember to look up all new terms and symbols in the "Dictionary of Musical Terms" on page 63.

11002A

Extension Study

(Extension between 1st and 2nd fingers)

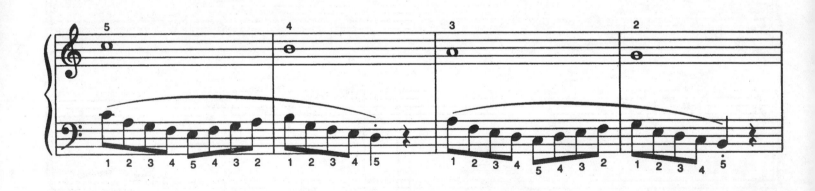

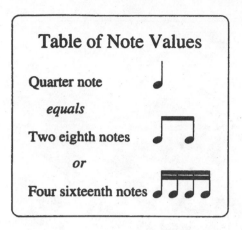

Study in Sixteenths

Each five note group under the slur should be played with one impulse. Practice with a high finger legato.

In a Goldfish Bowl

The ACCIACCATURA is a type of GRACE NOTE (♪) indicated by a small note with its stem crossed through. A grace note is usually played with a very light and quick motion. Think of the grace note as belonging to the note that follows it.

In this piece the grace notes should not be played too quickly because they are part of the melody.

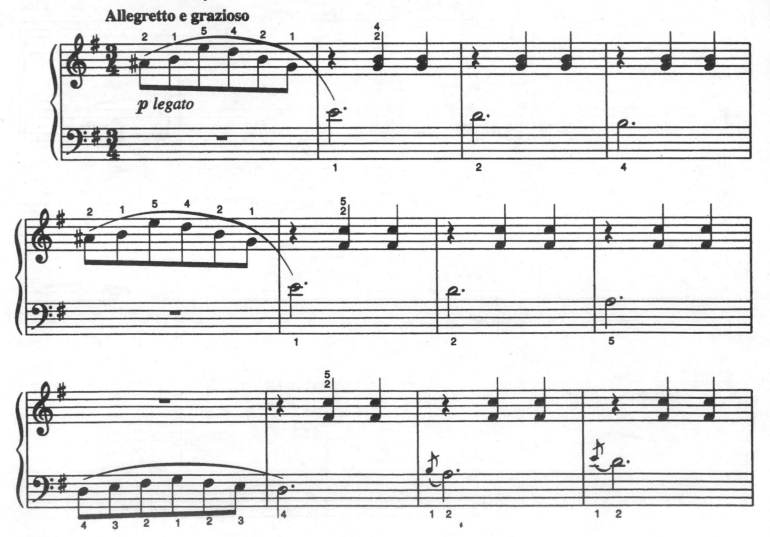

Extension Study
(Extension between 1st and 2nd, and 4th and 5th fingers)

Practice this study four ways.

1st – Hands separately, one note to the beat (quarter notes)

2nd – Hands separately, two notes to the beat (eighth notes)

3rd – Hands together, one note to the beat

4th – Hands together, two notes to the beat

HANON

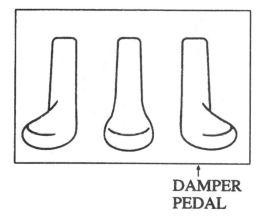

The Damper Pedal

The pedal on the right side is called the DAMPER PEDAL. The DAMPER PEDAL sustains tones.

Use your right foot to press the damper pedal down.

Keep your heel on the floor as your foot presses and releases the pedal.

DAMPER
PEDAL

Press the DAMPER PEDAL down and play the following notes.

Hold the pedal down and you will hear this chord.

The DAMPER PEDAL may also be used to connect tones as in the following:

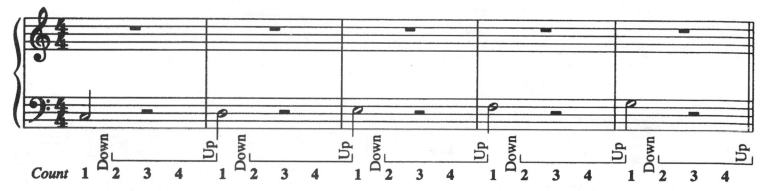

Press the damper pedal DOWN on count 2 and UP on count 1. Pedaling after the key has been struck is known as SYNCOPATED PEDALING and is used to give clarity to your playing and to avoid a sloppy effect of overlapping tones.

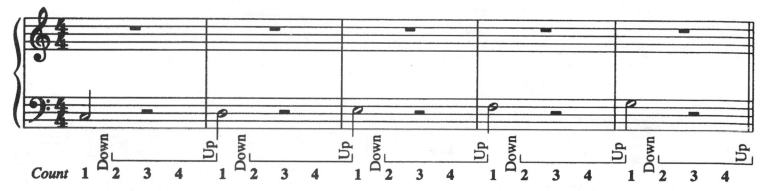

Dreamland

The use of the damper pedal will aid you in connecting the melody and will also provide a rich harmonic background. Be sure to pedal as marked.

The Dominant-Seventh Chord

Next to the TONIC CHORD (I) the DOMINANT-SEVENTH (V7) is the most important chord in harmonizing music.

With the use of these two chords, TONIC and DOMINANT-SEVENTH, it is possible to harmonize or form the accompaniment to many well known melodies and songs.

How to Form a Dominant-Seventh

Dominant on 5th note of scale

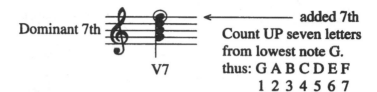

Dominant 7th

← added 7th
Count UP seven letters from lowest note G.
thus: G A B C D E F
     1 2 3 4 5 6 7

Here are the four positions of the DOMINANT-SEVENTH

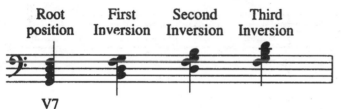

Here is the DOMINANT-SEVENTH an octave higher with the D omitted.

Practice the following accompaniment several times

Now play **Merrily We Roll Along**

Mer - ri - ly we roll a - long, roll a - long, roll a - long,

Mer - ri - ly we roll a - long, O'er the deep blue sea.

11002A

Forearm Staccato

HAND IN POSITION TO PLAY

DOWN ARM

UP ARM

At the Band Rehearsal

Moderato con brio

Play the chords with a forearm staccato touch.

mf *sempre staccato*

STEPHEN FOSTER (b. 1826 - d. 1864)

Stephen Foster is known as the greatest writer of American folk-songs. His melodies are simple, but very expressive, and will live as long as music is sung or played. Among his many famous songs, "Swanee River" is the most popular.

Swanee River

Play with expression and shade your melody.

Andante cantabile

STEPHEN FOSTER

'Way down up-on the Swa-nee Riv-er, Far, far a-way,

That's where my heart is turn-ing ev-er, That's where the old folks stay.

All the world is sad and drear-y, Ev-'ry-where I roam;

Oh, dar-ling, how my heart grows wear-y, Far from the old folks at home.

Sunrise

(Broken Chords)

The first note of each measure should be strongly accented. This will bring out the
HIDDEN MELODY. Use the DAMPER PEDAL as marked. Practice each three-
note group as a chord. This will give you additional chord practice and will also
help in attaining speed.

FRANZ SCHUBERT (b. 1797 - d. 1828)

Schubert was a great composer who might have risen to greater heights if death had not overtaken him at the early age of thirty-one. His "Unfinished Symphony" is a favorite among music lovers and possesses that haunting loveliness and purity which are characteristics of Schubert's music. He also created a new and distinctive form in song writing and will always be remembered for his many songs of rare beauty.

Unfinished Symphony

FRANZ SCHUBERT
arr. by Michael Aaron

Allegretto espressivo

Crossing the Thumb

THUMB ON C
2nd finger ready to play

2nd FINGER ON C♯
Thumb crossing UNDER

THUMB ON D

Chromatic Scale

The CHROMATIC SCALE is a series of twelve half-step intervals. A RELAXED THUMB will help you attain smooth crossings. Practice hands separately. This scale should be practiced daily.

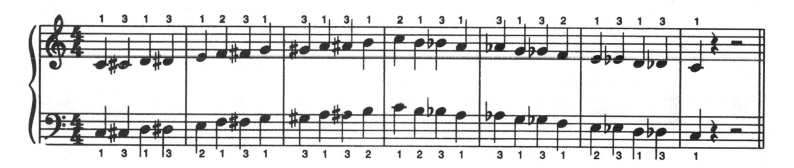

Study in Thumb Crossings

Practice hands separately and slowly. The speed may be increased gradually.

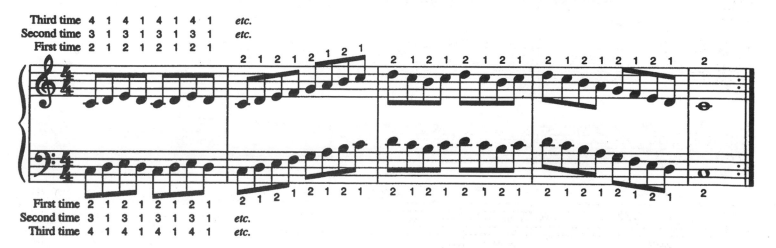

The Mosquito

(Thumb Crossings for Right Hand)

Notice the structure of this piece. It is composed of notes of the CHROMATIC SCALE. Play with a LIGHT and RELAXED THUMB. The first three measures suggest the humming sound of the mosquito and the fourth measure the "sting" and ensuing slap.

Allegretto

Cradle Song

(Thumb Crossings for Left Hand)

Try to "feel" the rocking of the cradle as you play the left hand. The upper dotted half notes of the right hand are MELODY NOTES and should be accented so that they may be heard above the left hand accompaniment.

Moderato

Note Reading Tests

(All Positions)

Spell the words by writing the correct letter name of each note.

To complete each test you must play the correct notes on the piano.

On Parade

Marches should always be played with well marked rhythm and accents. In $\frac{4}{4}$ time the FIRST BEAT or count is the strongest and is called the PRIMARY ACCENT. The next accent, falling on the THIRD BEAT or count, is called the SECONDARY ACCENT and is played with a lighter accent.

The Breakers

Have you spent a day at the sea shore? If you have, you probably experienced the thrill of the surging tide, as it rolled on to the beach and broke into countless white caps. Try to picture this when playing "The Breakers." The melody is in the treble staff and should be well accented. Use the pedal as indicated.

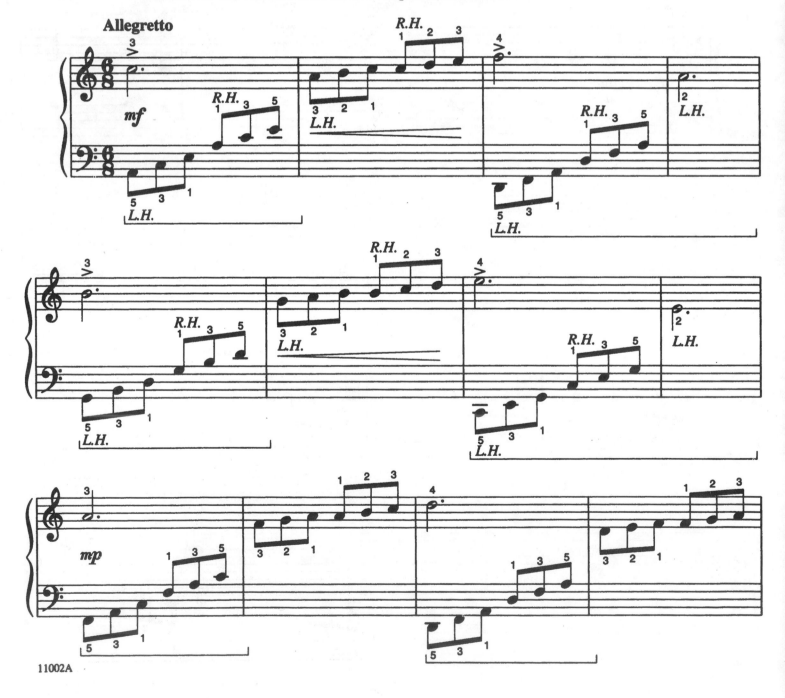

Note Reading Tests

(Four Positions)

Spell the following words with the correct notes in four positions on the staff.

Example

SPELL "FACE" in four positions

SPELL "CAGE" in four positions

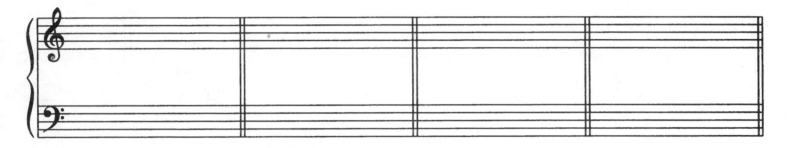

SPELL "DEAF" in four positions

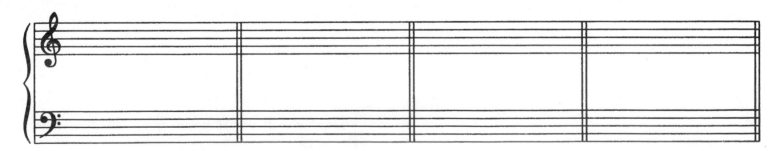

SPELL "BAG" in four positions

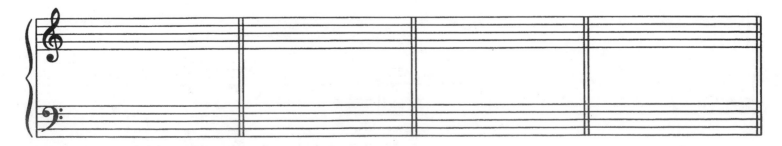

Chorale

Notice the new key signature A FLAT MAJOR. The four flats in this key are
B♭ E♭ A♭ D♭. Remember BEAD. Play the chords with a DOWN ARM touch
and strive for a full rich "organ tone."

Study in Triplets

Practice this study three ways.

1st – Finger 1-2-3 throughout
2nd – Finger 2-3-4 throughout
3rd – Finger 3-4-5 throughout

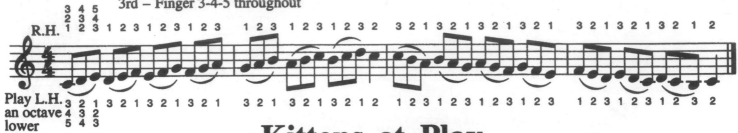

Kittens at Play

(Triplets)

The TRIPLETS (♪♪♪) in this piece are eighth notes and should be played three notes to the beat instead of the usual two. If you say the word "Won-der-ful" it will help you to feel the rhythm. Count in this manner ONE-der-ful, TWO-der-ful.

Allegretto

Minor Scale

The MINOR SCALE or KEY is often used to express sad or mysterious moods in musical composition. For example, play "Swanee River" in the key of C major:

Now play "Swanee River" in the key of C minor:

Notice how the FLATTED E and A change the mood of the piece to one of sadness.

Every MAJOR SCALE can be changed to a MINOR SCALE (harmonic form) by lowering the 3rd and 6th degrees a half step.

Example

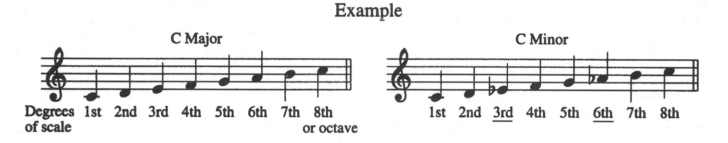

In the NATURAL FORM of the MINOR SCALE the 3rd, 6th and 7th degrees of the major scale are lowered a half step.

The LOWERED 3rd, 6th and 7th degrees E♭-A♭-B♭ are also found in the KEY of E FLAT MAJOR. Therefore C MINOR is called a RELATIVE of E FLAT MAJOR and has the same KEY SIGNATURE.

The 3rd degree of the MINOR SCALE will always give you the name of its RELATIVE MAJOR.

The 6th degree of the MAJOR SCALE will always give you the name of its RELATIVE MINOR.

Movie Thriller

Alphonse et Gaston

(Cross Hand)

Play this arrangement of a French Folk-tune in a lively manner. Study the first line thoroughly before practicing the cross hand part in the second line.

French Folk Tune

Allegretto

Intervals

An INTERVAL is the difference in pitch between two tones of the scale. Intervals are counted from the first note of the scale upwards. For example  is called a 3rd.

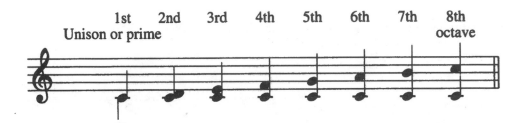

1st 2nd 3rd
do   re   mi

Intervals of the C Major Scale

1st   2nd   3rd   4th   5th   6th   7th   8th
Unison or prime   octave

Major and Minor Thirds

A MAJOR **3rd** is an interval of FOUR HALF STEPS.
A MINOR **3rd** is an interval of THREE HALF STEPS.

Here are the major and minor **3rds** built on each degree of the C Major scale.

MAJ. MIN. MIN. MAJ. MAJ. MIN. MIN. MAJ.

Any MAJOR **3rd** may be changed to a MINOR **3rd** by LOWERING the upper note a half step or RAISING the lower note a half step.

MAJ. MIN.

MAJ. MIN.

Any MINOR **3rd** may be changed to a MAJOR **3rd** by RAISING the upper note a half step or LOWERING the lower note a half step.

MIN. MAJ.

MIN. MAJ.

The Canary

(Trill Study)

To obtain an even trill you must practice slowly at first. Listen carefully to your playing and try to "match" each tone.

42

Wrist Staccato

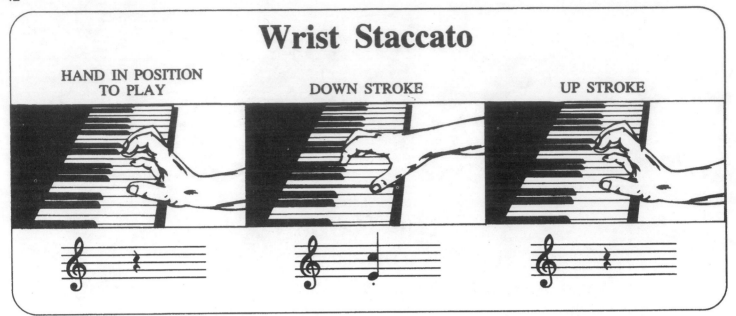

Study in Wrist Staccato

Major and Minor Sixths

A MAJOR SIXTH is an interval of NINE HALF STEPS.

A MINOR SIXTH is an interval of EIGHT HALF STEPS.

Here are the major and minor SIXTHS built on each degree of C MAJOR SCALE.

MAJ.   MAJ.   MIN.   MAJ.   MAJ.   MIN.   MIN.   MAJ.

Any MAJOR 6th may be changed to a MINOR
6th by LOWERING the upper note a half step
or RAISING the lower note a half step.

MAJ.   MIN.

MAJ.   MIN.

Any MINOR 6th may be changed to a MAJOR
6th by RAISING the upper note a half step or
LOWERING the lower note a half step.

MIN.   MAJ.

MIN.   MAJ.

JOHANNES BRAHMS (b. 1833 - d. 1897)

Brahms is regarded today as a great modern Master. His music is even called the music of the future. Brahms, the man, was very quiet and scholarly, and his own severest critic. He was very painstaking in his composing and therefore progressed slowly in order to attain perfection. Although a symphonist and composer of two piano concertos (in D minor and B flat major), both true masterpieces, Brahms also wrote many shorter works for the piano. Because of his brilliance, and creative imagination, he has been classified as one of the great "Three B's," of music, namely Bach, Beethoven and Brahms.

Waltz

In this lovely waltz by Brahms one feels the "floating" sway of the dancer. Follow the expression marks carefully.

JOHANNES BRAHMS
arr. by Michael Aaron

Teneramente e grazioso

11002A

Scale in Sixteenths

As a general rule INCREASE your tone gradually as you play UP the scale and DECREASE your tone as you play DOWN the scale.

The fifteenth measure of this study is an exception to this rule and should be played with a gradual decrescendo.

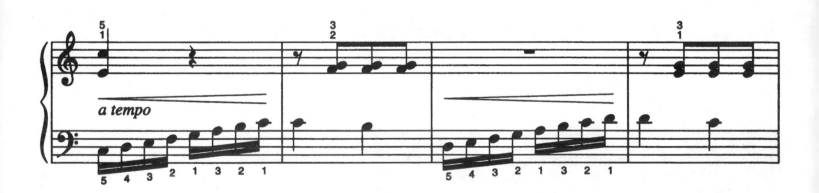

Fireflies
(Study in Style)

Play this piece with a light and "airy" touch. Notice that the left hand is played in the treble. All slur and staccato marks should be carefully observed. They add meaning and character to your playing.

Allegretto

11002A

Major and Minor Triads

We learned the three MAJOR TRIADS of the major scale in GRADE ONE.

(do) TONIC	(sol) DOMINANT	(fa) SUB-DOMINANT
I	V	IV

Now we will study the three MINOR TRIADS on the 2nd, 3rd, and 6th degrees of the major scale.

(re) SUPER-TONIC	(mi) MEDIANT	(la) SUB-MEDIANT
II	III	IV

Major and Minor Triads of C Major Scale

MAJ.	MIN.	MIN.	MAJ.	MAJ.	MIN.		MAJ.
I	II	III	IV	V	VI	VII	I

Any MAJOR TRIAD may be changed to a MINOR TRIAD by LOWERING THE **3rd** of the chord a half step.

MAJ.   MIN.

Any MINOR TRIAD may be changed to a MAJOR TRIAD by RAISING THE **3rd** of the chord a half step.

MIN.   MAJ.

Teacher: Major and minor triads of other scales may be introduced at the discretion of the teacher.

*The DIMINISHED TRIAD is explained in MICHAEL AARON PIANO COURSE, GRADE THREE.

The Old Tar

All sixteenth notes should be practiced at three different speeds.

1st as quarter notes, one note to a count.
2nd as eighth notes, two notes to a count.
3rd as sixteenth notes, four notes to a count.

On Wings of Song

The melody of this beautiful song by Mendelssohn rises above the smooth even flowing accompaniment of the left hand. Shade the accompaniment as well as the melody.

F. MENDELSSOHN (B. 1809-D. 1847)

arr. by Michael Aaron

Andante cantabile

JOHANN SEBASTIAN BACH (b. 1685 - d. 1750)

Although Bach lived and composed in the early Eighteenth Century, his music possesses that immortal quality which belongs to all ages. Bach has often been called a "musician's musician," and rightly so, since his music proved to be a source of inspiration to many of the great composers. The student will also derive much benefit from the study of Bach, which is so helpful in training the fingers and the mind. Bach wove his melodies into beautiful designs in much the same manner as a master weaver of carpets. His "Twenty-four Preludes and Fugues" in all keys is one of the great contributions to the development of music.

Minuet

To make your playing of "Minuet" more expressive, be sure to "shade" the melody. One simple rule to remember is to INCREASE the tone when the melody goes UP ⟨ and DECREASE the tone when the melody goes DOWN ⟩.

J. S. BACH

Jig

Rhythm has often been called the "Heart Beat of Music." Without rhythm music is lifeless. In "Jig" the first and fourth beats are strongly accented. Play as rapidly as possible; however, do not sacrifice clarity for speed.

Allegro con brio

LUDWIG *van* BEETHOVEN (b. 1770 - d. 1827)

Beethoven's music possesses a lofty and noble character. His piano sonatas and symphonies rank among the world's greatest music literature. Despite being handicapped by deafness in his later years, it was then that he composed some of his best music. This shining example shows how one can overcome even the greatest of handicaps if the ambition and desire is strong enough.

Turkish March

In this march by Beethoven you can hear the footsteps of the soldiers in the distance. As they come closer and closer the music increases in volume. Play the grace notes with a light touch.

LUDWIG van BEETHOVEN
arr. by Michael Aaron

The Whistler

Blessings on thee, little man,
Barefoot boy, with cheeks of tan,
With thy turned-up pantaloons,
And thy merry whistled tunes.

Whittier

Allegretto

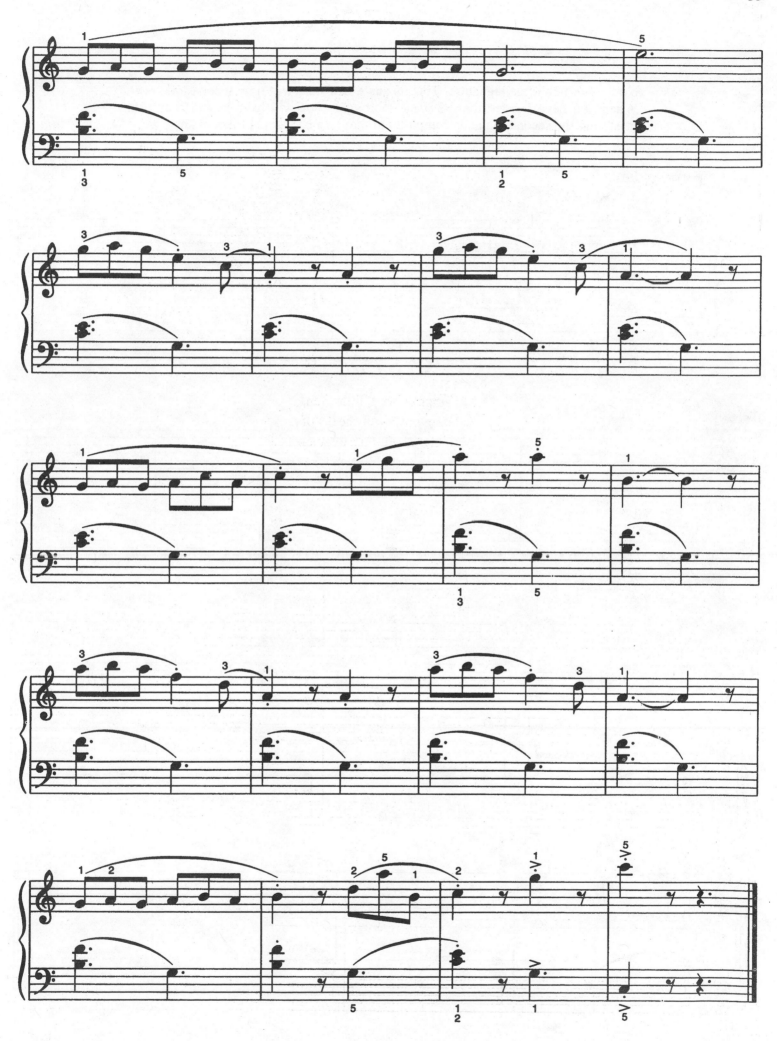

Prelude

Notice the new time signature. This means a half note will now receive one beat. When you have learned the first page thoroughly you will have less difficulty in mastering the second which is composed of the same chords in broken form.

Tarantella

The name TARANTELLA is derived from a poisonous spider called a tarantula. The victims of this poisonous spider were said to be imbued with a wild desire to leap into the air and dance for hours.

Be sure to play "Tarantella" with strong rhythm and well marked accents on FIRST and FOURTH beats.

In the Toy Shop

This piece describes a scene in a toy shop. See if you can guess which musical instrument is being imitated.

8va - - - - - means play an octave higher.

Major Scales and Major Triads

Major Scales and Major Triads

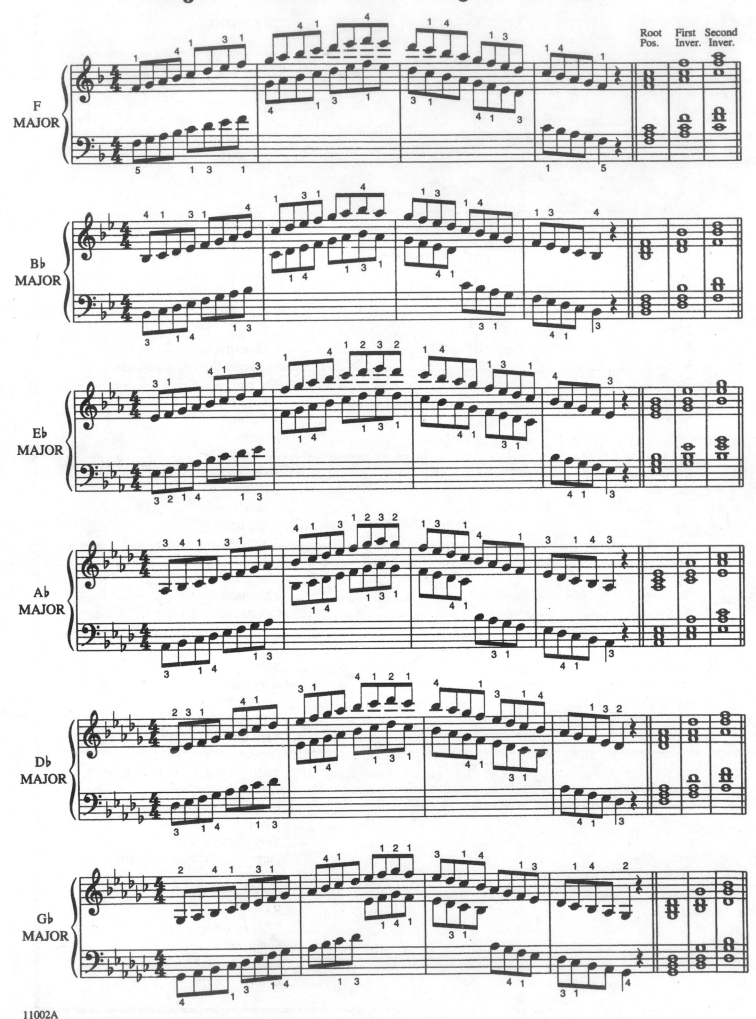

DICTIONARY OF MUSICAL TERMS

MUSICAL TERM	ABBREVIATION or SIGN	MEANING
A Tempo	*A tempo*	On time
Accelerando	*Accel.*	Increase speed gradually
Accent Mark	>	Accent note
Agitato	*Agitato*	Agitated
Alla Marcia	*Alla marcia*	In march style
Allegretto	*Allegretto*	Merrily (fairly rapid)
Allegro	*Allegro*	Fast
Andante	*Andante*	Slowly
Animato	*Animato*	With spirit, lively
Cantabile	*Cantabile*	In a singing or vocal style
Con brio	*Con brio*	With spirit
Crescendo	*Cresc.* <	Gradually louder
Da Capo	*D.C.*	Return to the beginning
Decrescendo	*Decresc.* >	Gradually softer
Diminuendo	*Dim.*	Softer by degrees
Dolce	*Dolce*	Sweetly
Espressivo	*Espressivo*	With expression
Fermata	⌢	Hold note longer than its actual value
Fine	*Fine*	The end
Forte	f	Loud
Fortissimo	$f\!f$	Very loud
Grazioso	*Grazioso*	Gracefully
Il Canto	*Il Canto*	The melody
Left Hand	*L.H.*	To be played by the left hand
La Melodia	*La Melodia*	The melody
Legato	*Legato*	Smooth and connected
Leggiero	*Leggiero*	Light and airy
Lento	*Lento*	A little slower than andante
Marcato	*Marcato*	Play with emphasis
Mezzo-forte	*mf*	Moderately loud
Mezzo-piano	*mp*	Moderately soft
Misterioso	*Misterioso*	In a mysterious manner
Moderato	*Moderato*	Moderate rate of speed (not too fast)
Molto vivace	*Molto Vivace*	Very lively
Piano	p	Soft
Pianissimo	*pp*	Very soft
Poco a poco	*Poco a poco*	By degrees
Poco moto	*Poco Moto*	A little motion
Presto	*Presto*	Very fast
Repeat Sign	𝄇	Repeat
Right Hand	*R.H.*	To be played with the right hand
Ritard	*rit.*	Gradually slower
Scherzando	*Scherzando*	In a playful manner
Sempre	*Sempre*	Always
Sforzando	*sfz*	Very strong accent
Simile	*simile*	Same as indicated previously
Slight Accent	–	Sustain
Staccato	*Stacc.*	Detached, short
Tempo	*Tempo*	Rate of speed
Teneramente	*Teneramente*	With tender emotion
Tranquillo	*Tranquillo*	Quiet, calm
Vivace	*Vivace*	Fast and Lively
Vivo	*Vivo*	Lively, briskly

Certificate

of

Achievement

This certifies that

---

has successfully completed
Grade Two of
The Michael Aaron Piano Course
and is now ready to begin
Grade Three

The
Michael
Aaron
Piano
Course

_____

Teacher

_____

Date